CONTENTS

Part 1 - Starting Your Credit Journey (Beginners)

1. Understanding Credit Scores

2. Building/Managing Credit

3. Establishing Credit

Part 2 - Building Credit After Bankruptcy

1. Recovering from Bankruptcy

2. Rebuilding Strategies

3. Apply For New Credit

Part 1
Starting Your Credit Journey

"You're embarking on an exciting journey towards financial empowerment! Stay committed to your goals, and watch as your credit journey unfolds into success!"

Understanding Credit Scores

Your credit score is your financial reputation. This score will be a important key factor to gaining the trust of lendors, landlords, jobs and the ability to borrow money. A credit score is unique to you. Understanding this three-digit number can help you unlock financial opportunities.

What is a Credit Score?

A credit score is like a report card for grown-ups, grading you based off on time payments, and how you handle money. Think of it as a game, where you wanna score as many points as possible to unlock low interest rates, bigger loans and other cool rewards. Scores typically range from 300 to 850, with higher scores indicating lower credit risk.

Components of a Credit Score

Payment History (35%)

It tracks whether you pay your bills on time, including credit cards, loans, and mortgages. When you pay on time consistently, you have now proven you are reliable. Lendors will be anxious to offer you money.

Credit Utilization (30%)

This measures how much of your available credit you're using. Aim to keep the balance below 30% to show lenders you can manage credit responsibly. They will be impressed.

Length of Credit History (15%)

The longer your credit history, the better. It includes how long your accounts have been open and the average age of your accounts. Its like building a relationship of financial trust.

Credit Mix (10%)

Lenders like to see a mix of credit types, such as credit cards, installment loans, and mortgages. Secure and non secured credit cards. Store cards and banking credit cards.

New Credit (10%)

Don't go overboard with too many credit applications. You dont want to look risky! Focus on building steadily. Opening multiple new accounts in a short time can signal financial stress and lower your score temporarily.

For a six-month credit-building goal, I'd recommend applying for no more than two or three credit accounts. This allows you to establish a solid foundation without overwhelming yourself or appearing too eager to lenders. Remember, patience is key when building credit!

How Credit Scores Impact You

Loan Approval

Lenders use your credit score to determine whether to approve your loan application. Higher scores typically mean better loan terms and lower interest rates.

Credit Card Rates

A good score can lead to high credit limits and lower interest rates on credit cards, potentially saving you money in the long run.

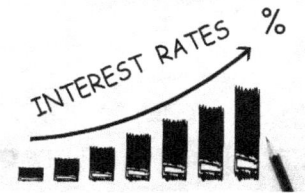

An **interest rate** is like a fee you pay for borrowing money. When you borrow money, like taking out a loan or using a credit card, the lender charges you interest on top of the amount you borrowed. The lower the interest rate, the less money you have to pay back.

Insurance Premiums

Some insurance companies use credit scores to set premiums. A higher score may mean lower insurance costs.

Renting a Home

Landlords often check credit scores to determine rental approval. A strong score can improve your chances of getting that dream apartment with little to no deposit. Lower scores usually get tenants denied or a increased rental deposit.

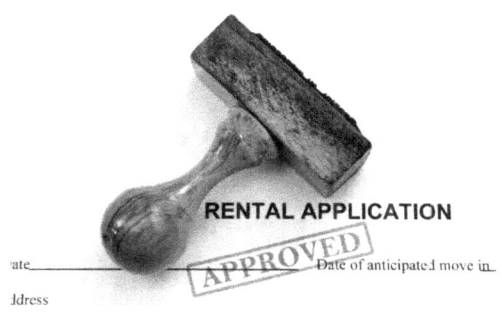

Establishing Credit

The quickest and simplest way to establish credit for beginners is to get a secured credit card. Here's how it works:

Apply for a Secured Credit Card

Secured cards are designed for those with little to no credit history. They require a security deposit, which also acts as your credit limit.

Make Small Purchases

Once you have the card, use it to make small, regular purchases that you can easily afford to pay off each month.

Pay On Time, Every Time

The most important step is to pay your credit card bill on time and in full every month.

After you have made 2-3 payments towards a secured card a company will start to be more easygoing.

Secured card : A secured card is the blueprint for beginners credit. You put down a deposit as collateral, ($50-$250) which becomes your credit limit. It's a great way to build credit if you're just starting or rebuilding from past mistakes.

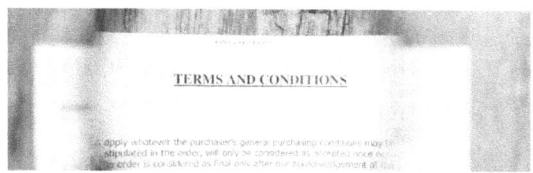

*Most companies will refund your deposit. Read the terms and conditions. There is alot of hidden benefits and savings.

Now that you showed you can make on time payments, apply for a unsecured card.

Unsecured card : with a unsecured card there's no deposit required. Your credit limit is based on your creditworthiness and financial history.

Here are a few credit card companies known for being beginner-friendly to those with less-than-perfect credit:

Discover it® Secured Credit Card:

Great for beginners, offers cashback rewards and doesn't require a minimum credit score.

Capital One Platinum Secured Credit Card:

Another solid option for building credit. It has no annual fee and offers a path to a higher credit limit with responsible card use.

I started my credit building journey with a secured capital one card. A $100 deposit got me a $251 credit limit. Once i paid on this card for 3 months, I then applied for their Platinum unsecured card. I was approved and given a $500 credit limit. No deposit necessary. This was the start to my 700+ journey.

Compare rates, fees, and benefits to find the best fit for your financial situation!

Chase Freedom Flex℠:

Offers cash back rewards and benefits, accessible to those with fair credit.

Bank of America® Travel Rewards Credit Card:

Good for beginners who want a travel rewards card without an annual fee.

Citi® Secured Mastercard®:

Another secured card option to build credit, with no annual fee.

Building Your Credit Score

Stay on Top of Bills!

Consistently paying bills on time is the most effective way to boost your score.

Keep Balances Low!

Don't max out your cards. Keeping a low balance can improve your credit utilization. It shows you are responsible.

Diversify Your Credit!

Mix it up! Apply for different types of credit. Start with a secured card, after 2 or 3 payments apply for a unsecured card with the same company. See if you are pre-approved, then try a personal loan from a credit union. Variety is the spice of credit life!

Part 2
Building Credit After Bankruptcy

"Embrace your fresh start. Starting to build credit after bankruptcy can feel like climbing a mountain. Think of it as hitting the rest button on your financial future.

By taking proactive steps to rebuild your credit, you're showing determination, and a commitment."

Recovering from Bankruptcy

Check Your Credit Report

• Ensure all debts are discharged and correctly marked as "discharged" or "included in bankruptcy." All discharged items should show as $0.

• Dispute any inaccuracies or errors on your credit report.

Create a Solid Plan

• Take a detailed look at your financial situation post-bankruptcy.

• Create a budget that tracks your income and expenses.

• Understand where your money is going and identify areas where you can cut back or save.

Establish an Emergency Fund

- Aim to save at least three to six months' worth of living expenses.

- This fund will help prevent relying on credit for unexpected expenses and provide a financial safety net.

Freeze Third Party Consumer Reports

There are many companies that may keep financial records, including bank info, public records, and other financial data.

I have included a list of third party companies you may need to freeze, or dispute.

Consumer reporting agencies:

1. **ChexSystems:**

Provides reports related to checking and savings account activity, including negative information such as bounced checks and overdrafts.

2. **CoreLogic Teletrack**:

Specializes in providing reports on consumers' banking and lending history, particularly subprime lending data.
- Website: [CoreLogic Teletrack] (https://www.corelogic.com/solutions/teletrack.aspx)

3. **Risk Solutions**:

Provides risk assessment and identity verification services, including financial history data from public records.
- Website: [LexisNexis Risk Solutions] (https://risk.lexisnexis.com/products)

4. **MicroBilt**:

Offers credit and identity verification services, including access to alternative credit data and public records.
- Website: [MicroBilt](https://www.microbilt.com/)

5. **Early Warning Services**:

Provides fraud prevention and risk management solutions for financial institutions, including checking account verification services.
- Website: [Early Warning Services](https://www.earlywarning.com/)

6. **National Consumer Telecom & Utilities Exchange (NCTUE)**:

Maintains data on telecommunications and utility accounts, including payment history and account status.
- Website: [NCTUE](https://www.nctue.com/)

7. **SageStream**:

Offers consumer credit reporting services, including non-traditional credit data and public records.
- Websitte: [SageStream] (https://www.sagestreamllc.com/)

8. **Clarity Services** (a part of Experian):

Provides alternative credit data, including payday loans and other non-traditional credit information.
- Website: [Clarity Services] (https://www.clarityservices.com/)

9. **FactorTrust** (a part of TransUnion):

Offers alternative credit data and risk management solutions for lenders.
- Website: [FactorTrust] (https://www.factortrust.com/)

10. **Innovis**:

Provides consumer credit reports and identity verification services, particularly for smaller financial institutions.
- Website: [Innovis](https://www.innovis.com/)

Please note that while these agencies may maintain financial records, not all of them provide access to consumers for the purpose of freezing or disputing information.

Rebuilding Strategies:

1. Get a Secured Credit Card

A secured credit card is often the easiest type of credit to get after bankruptcy. You'll need to make a deposit, which becomes your credit limit. Pay the balance in full every month.

2. Apply for a Credit-Builder Loan

Some credit unions and banks offer credit-builder loans. These loans are designed to help you build credit. You make small monthly payments, and once the loan is paid off, you receive the money back.

3. Become an Authorized User

If a family member or friend with good credit is willing to add you as an authorized user on their credit card, it can help establish positive credit history for you. Just make sure the primary cardholder uses the card responsibly.

4. Negotiate with Creditors

Contact creditors of reaffirmed debts from your bankruptcy and negotiate for more favorable terms, such as reduced balances or interest rates. Paying off these debts can positively impact your credit score.

Request a pay to delete only with the original creditor. Get a email statement agreeing to this before making a payment.

5. Explore Alternative Credit Data:

Sign up for services that report rent payments, utility bills, and cell phone payments.

6. Apply for a Retail Store Card:

Retail store credit cards often have lower approval requirements, making them easier for individuals with less-than-perfect credit.

7. Consider a Peer-to-Peer Loan:

Peer-to-peer lending platforms connect borrowers with individual investors willing to fund loans. These loans may have more lenient credit requirements than traditional lenders.

8. Focus on Credit Mix:

In addition to revolving credit accounts like credit cards, consider diversifying your credit mix by adding installment loans, such as a personal loan or auto loan.

9. Make Timely Payments

Pay all bills, not just credit card billes, on time. Payment history makes up a significant portion of your credit score, so it's crucial to demonstrate a pattern of timely payments.

Create a alert on your phone calendar to pay your bills monthly.

Create this alert to notify you 3 days ahead of payment due. This gives you time to assess your finances and get the amount due.

Create a second alert for the day ahead of your bill payment.

If you can pay early, do so!

Take the time to setup this reoccurring alert for every month of the year.

Apply For New Credit

After bankruptcy, some credit cards are more likely to approve applicants who are working on rebuilding their credit.

Secured Credit Cards:

-Discover it® Secured Credit Card: This card offers cash back rewards, and after 8 months, Discover automatically reviews your account to see if you can transition to an unsecured card.

- Capital One Secured Mastercard: No annual fee and a minimum security deposit requirement. Capital One also offers the opportunity to increase your credit limit with responsible card use.

- Citi® Secured Mastercard®: This card is designed for individuals looking to build or rebuild credit. It has no annual fee and reports to all three major credit bureaus.

Credit Builder Cards:

Petal® 2 "Cash Back, No Fees" Visa® Credit Card:

This card is designed for those with limited credit history or rebuilding credit. It offers cash back rewards and does not require a security deposit.

OpenSky® Secured Visa® Credit Card:

No credit check is required for approval, making it accessible for those with poor or no credit history. It reports to all three major credit bureaus.

Credit Builder Loans:

- Self Credit Builder Account: Not a traditional credit card, but it helps you build credit by making small monthly payments into a CD, which you receive back at the end of the term.

Store Credit Cards:

Amazon Store Card:

This card is easier to qualify for and can help rebuild credit. It can only be used at Amazon but offers special financing options for eligible purchases.

Target REDcard™:

Another store card option, it provides a discount on Target purchases and reports to the major credit bureaus.

Fingerhut Credit Account:

Often more lenient in their approval process and can help rebuild credit.

Macy's Credit Card:

Macy's offers a store card that can be easier to qualify for post-bankruptcy.

Synchrony Bank backed store credit cards.

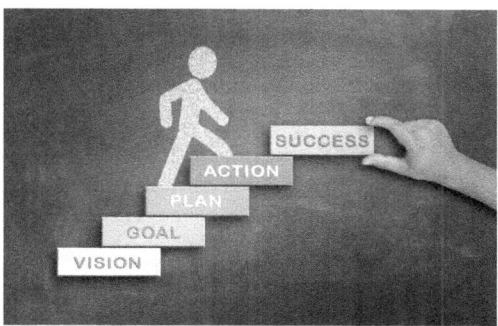

Subprime Credit Cards:

Indigo® Platinum Mastercard®:

Designed for those with less-than-perfect credit. While it has an annual fee, it can be a stepping stone to better credit if used responsibly.

In conclusion, for beginners and those who have recently filed bankruptcy, building credit starts with understanding your credit report, opening new accounts responsibly, making timely payments, and keeping balances low.

Additionally, after bankruptcy, focus on rebuilding slowly. Use secured cards or credit-builder loans, and monitor your progress.

With patience and discipline, anyone can improve their credit score over time.

Website links to all three major credit bureaus:

Equifax: - Website: [Equifax Credit Monitoring] (https://www.equifax.com/personal/credit-report-services/credit-monitoring/)

Experian: - Website: [Experian Credit Monitoring] (https://www.experian.com/consumer-products/credit-monitoring.html)

TransUnion: - Website: [TransUnion Credit Monitoring] (https://www.transunion.com/credit-monitoring)

Biography

"In this empowering ebook, I've shared with you the keys to unlock a world of financial freedom and prosperity.

As a seasoned expert in the realm of credit management, I've dedicated my career to guiding individuals like you towards a brighter financial future.

Get ready to embark on a journey of self-discovery, empowerment, and lasting prosperity."

-Antonionia Marie

www.ingramcontent.com/pod-product-compliance
Lightning Source LLC
Chambersburg PA
CBHW062208220526
45470CB00009B/2973